Faith House

A Journey to Faith

Pat Farrell

To God be the
glory!

Pat
Farrell

Faith House: A Journey to Faith by Patricia Farrell

Published by PatFarrell,LLC
5525 Lead Mine Road Hiwassee, Virginia 24347
ISBN: 978-0-69209338-2
Copyright © 2018 by Patricia Farrell
Cover Design by For the Muse Design
Interior design by AtriTeX Technologies Private Ltd, Chennai, India

Available in print from www.patfarrellcoach.com

For more information on this book and the author visit:
www.patfarrellcoach.com

Editor: Barbara Dick

Library of Congress Cataloging-in-Publication Data

Farrell, Patricia

Faith House: A Journey to Faith / Patricia Farrell, 1st ed.

Printed in the United States of America

This book is dedicated to the Glory of God and all the women who enter the doors of Faith House. The story could not be told without the forgiveness and love of my daughter, and the support and encouragement of my husband. Without them, I would not be where I am today, and for that I give thanks to God.

Preface

If I had known Jesus, I might not have drunk so much. I wouldn't have spent my life searching for something or someone to fill my big empty hole. I would not have stayed in a loveless marriage or needed to have affairs. If I had known Jesus, I would not have suffered from anorexia and bulimia, over-exercised, over-worked, or over-compensated.

But it was in the desert of my life—on my knees . . . not in a time of joy . . . not in church or in celebration, but in defeat . . . in submission . . . in grief and surrender— that I found Jesus Christ; that He showed up in my life. When everybody else walked out, Jesus walked in.

It has been a slow but steady walk out of the desert of my life. I lived much of my life in a place of numbing denial, a spiritual desert, unable to deal with the pain of reality. I went to church. I showed up every Sunday and sat in my familiar pew, but I did not know God. I heard all the stories of Jesus. I saw the baby in the manger, I saw the body on the cross, but I had no clue. I did not know Him. And even though I lived day to day with no knowledge of His presence—He was always there.

The idea of writing a book has been nudging and whispering to me for years. I may not know "how" to write a book, I certainly know what to say. There are so many stories out there. But here is my headline:

*Y*ou Are Not Alone!

Thousands share your story. Some folks may be a little bit ahead of you on the path, but because of the path, they can hold a flashlight for you to find your way. I want you to see where we have been and where we don't want you to go.

You have no shame. You and I are forgiven. Jesus said, "Go, and sin no more" (John 8:11 KJV). Hold your head high and march forward, knowing that the Holy Spirit of God will love and guide you every step of the way. He promised to never leave or forsake you. Believe Him and allow Him to lead you out of your despair. There is a wonderful world of peace and purpose waiting for you!

You won't need any drugs or alcohol. You can stop that compulsive handwashing and counting. You can fearlessly get on a plane or mingle in a crowd at the mall. You can walk away from a relationship founded and fed in darkness. Turn your soul toward His eternal light and feel a love so profound that you will awaken from within.

As you read these words, know that I am praying for you. And know that I have no doubt of your healing because "nothing will be impossible with God" (Luke 1:37 ESV). He, in His immeasurable power, will work miracles in and through you. And the world is just waiting to see the glory of Him as revealed in YOU!

It is my prayer that through sharing my journey you come to realize—in any situation of your life—God is always with you. We are companions on the journey.

May your eyes and ears be opened so that you can behold His presence in your everyday life.

God bless you and keep you. May He shine His love around you and bring you peace.

Introduction: Faith House

*"Create a place for women to come—a nurturing place
. . . a trusting place."*

Sitting at the kitchen table, these are the words I heard in
my heart. They came so profoundly that I could hardly write
them fast enough. Sometimes soulful thoughts come on
the wind of an energy that is not of my own. You will know
that force when it comes to you—in time—as you open
your soul to listening.

Create a place? What place? Where? I didn't know
what God had planned, and, while it was not time for
me to know, I held on to those words. Days, months,
and years went by.

The phone rang. A realtor called: "I think I found a
place that you and your husband would like." She didn't
know about those other words spoken to me. She
didn't know my passion or purpose. She knew only that
I love rivers, lakes, and streams.

We pulled up to this old house and . . . my heart
flipped. Pay attention when you get the heart flip! It's
that sudden burst of joy or excitement when you see
something or hear something, and somehow you know
in your heart it is meant for you.

I got out of the car and stood in silence. "This is
the house! This is the Lord's house, the place that He

spoke to me." Standing quietly on a hill above a rolling river, the house looked like an old company store. With massive windows and open shutters, she held a mystery yet to be unveiled.

I stepped inside, speechless. I had never seen such crown molding. Her floors were warm and inviting, marked with the steps of thousands who must have entered her doors. While her physical beauty was inspiring, it was the spirituality of the house that was so overwhelming. Truly the spirit of the Lord moved in this house. There was stillness . . . a peace that transcends all understanding that was woven throughout her rooms.

It has been quite a journey coming to this "Faith House." I'm not sure when I realized I was even on the trip. It has been a gradual transformation to this place of understanding of who I am and the purpose in life God has chosen for me. God can take your past and use it to help people who cross your path.

How did Faith House come to be? Why would God call someone like me? This is my story of how God can take anybody and use them to further His kingdom. Come on this journey with me. Look and see what God can do with the likes of someone like me.

~ 1 ~

In the beginning God created the heavens and the earth. Now the earth was formless and empty, darkness was over the surface of the deep, and the Spirit of God was hovering over the waters.

—Genesis 1:1-2

I was born with a very large, flat, red birthmark called a port wine stain. It starts on the left side of my neck and covers the upper part of my chest, shoulder, and most of my left arm, hand, and fingers. I can remember that no matter how hot it would be outside, I always wore a turtleneck or a long-sleeved cotton shirt buttoned to the top.

People would ask my daddy about "it," and they would talk over and around me as if I weren't standing there: "What's wrong with her?" "It's just a birthmark," he would respond. How could anyone love me with this terrible disfigurement?

We didn't have fancy camouflage creams back then. And, for years after they came on the market, they were messy, with terribly fake colors. It was just easier to wear the long sleeves and pretend you were cold (even when sweat was running down your face).

Even though I have said "it doesn't bother me as a grown woman," I guess my actions have demonstrated something different. Several years ago, I had much of the birthmark removed with a yellow dye laser at Duke University. Even today, I will never buy an off-the-shoulder dress. I get a little embarrassed when someone asks about my "sunburn" or "skin rash"; "What's wrong with your neck?" Most are so embarrassed to have asked that I actually feel worse for them than I do for me.

If it wasn't my birthmark, surely it was something in my childhood that caused my incredible insecurity. Life seemed so normal. I love to remember and even write about the "normal" times I had in my life. I want them to overshadow the sad parts.

A 1950s childhood was all about a Tiny Tears doll, catching fireflies, and playing kick the can. I loved that Tiny Tears doll, and still find myself searching the Internet for an old one. Flat pink ears and painted on rubber swirls for hair; she came in a pink "carry case," with little frilly dresses, white folded cloth diapers, and little black shoes. I carried that doll until her arm fell off—literally.

My family always had a real Christmas tree with paper-thin shiny balls and big, bold-colored bulbs that got so hot you couldn't touch them. I don't know how we didn't burn the house down during the holidays.

Strands of silver tinsel hung from each tree branch. One year, we switched to "bubble lights." They were always orange and green, and the tiny bubbles would flow through the cylinder tube to the end. They never worked for long, so we had to keep an extra supply of replacements on hand.

We always went to my grandmother's house for Christmas supper (not dinner, but supper). She made steak and gravy, and she made buttermilk biscuits in a wooden bowl. Never measuring any ingredients, she would knead the mixture and pinch off the dough to make the most perfect biscuits. Lightly pressing them down with the back side of her fingers, her final touch was a tad of buttermilk smeared right on top. They were always identical and the perfect three inches in diameter. Soft and creamy, you could taste the tang of the buttermilk on your tongue.

My parents both worked—long and hard. They were mill workers. We lived in a modest "cotton mill house." If you are from the South, you know what I mean. Readers from coal country can relate to it too. It's the same as a "coal mining house." If you were raised on the golf course or spent summers abroad, I can describe it for you: it was a four-room house that, when you stood in the middle, you could see all four rooms.

When I was a teenager, my daddy added on his "TV room." We would watch *Gunsmoke* and *The Rifleman*. His little space didn't have much insulation, so we moved to the living room in the cold of winter.

We went to Myrtle Beach every summer during the July 4th holiday—for a week! That's when the mills shut down. My family (cousins and aunts included) drove station wagons and would sit in line for hours waiting to get into Myrtle Beach State Park. It was blazing hot, but we didn't seem to mind. Camping is so much fun when you're a kid. You don't have to do any of the work! We would fight over who would get the jungle hammocks; we only had two of them, so we had to take turns sleeping in them. The hammocks had a top cover and mesh netting on the sides, and it felt so cool and dark on the inside. I'd zip myself up and settle in for the night.

Oh, the smell of the bacon and eggs first thing in the morning! And I will always remember my daddy's grilled, buttered toast. For the life of me, I can't make it to taste the way it did when we camped. It must be the outdoors or the flame of that old gas grill that gave it such a nostalgic flavor.

> *I asked myself, "Why are you writing about camping in a tale of getting to Faith House?" And when I realized the truth, I began to cry. I could not hold back the tears. It has been fifty-five years, and I am still healing. I didn't even know I had any pain until I realized camping is one happiness from my childhood that I want to hold onto. It was a time of laughing and playing with no darkness or dread of loneliness.*

Some 1950s television programs depicted a father, mother, white picket fence, a brother or sister, and a family pet—all happy and smiling. That must be normal. I wanted normal. I wanted that cherry pink and apple blossom white in my life. I'm holding on to those memories of camping. I have to include them. They are my normal.

~ 2 ~

There is one whose rash words are like sword thrusts,
but the tongue of the wise brings healing.
—Proverbs 12:18 ESV

It's a long way from my grandmother's house to "that boy's house" over by the boat-landing road . . . especially on a bike . . . especially for a ten-year-old.

Jimmy was a handsome one, and older. He had tanned skin and sandy blond hair. Even though I was only ten years old, I wondered how I could get his attention. My parents were good friends with his mom and dad. I remember he had a cute younger brother too, who was closer to my age, but I wasn't after *his* attention.

My mother's hairdresser lived on the same boat-landing road. I would always ride with Mama to get her hair shampooed and styled . . . just in case I got a glimpse of Jimmy. I craved his attention.

I rode my bike all the way over there and didn't get to see Jimmy; but did I take the wrath from one of my relatives: "Boy crazy. She's just boy crazy." I was so humiliated and ashamed. Those words hurt me as much today as they did fifty years ago. Those words still bring up such shame. Be tender with children. You never know how your words will stay with them the rest of their life.

I must have been quite a spectacle; so desperate for attention. "Who is going to love me?" must have been written across my forehead. I had no clue who I was, no thought of self-fulfillment or self-love. Gifts? Talents? It had never crossed my mind that God had anything special for me to do in my life. Purpose? Seriously? Was God even aware of me? Who was this God anyway? He's up in heaven, and I am way down here on earth. Who is to blame for all of my inadequacies? Surely there is something or someone that I can hold responsible for my failures. All I knew was I had to find somebody to love me.

~ 3 ~

Then the LORD spoke to you out of the fire. You heard the sound of words, but saw no form; there was only a voice.
—Deuteronomy 4:12

I wonder if most kids had parents who had to work odd shifts. One went in at 7:00 AM and worked until 3:00 PM; the other from 3:00 PM until 11:00 PM. They carried their lunch or dinner in small brown sacks that we called "pokes." I can remember being handed off from one to the other at shift time in the mill parking lot. They really did the best they could.

My mama was tired and tried to please everybody. She struggled to climb the ladder of success in the mill. She became the first female floor supervisor. The women hated her, and she would come home and cry.

Mama adored my older cousin. And I'm betting everybody out there has had someone in his or her life who is forever that unattainable model of perfection. As hard as I tried, I would never grow to be 5' 10", slim and beautiful. Oh, how Mama wanted me to be as smart as my cousin was, and she would often make hurtful comparisons. I failed miserably to measure up. Mama would buy my clothes; I will never forget this horrible patchwork full-skirted dress she brought home one day. It was hideous, but Mama beamed and pleaded,

"But your cousin has one just like it!" Then I hated it more. It probably looked incredible on her, but it made me look like a Scottie dog.

I remember my mama holding onto a tall wardrobe and crying—actually sobbing—over my embarrassing her. I don't remember the incident. Must have been something I said or didn't say. Did or didn't do. To bring your mother to tears like that makes you feel so worthless.

You don't have to be physically abused to be damaged goods. You can just be a disappointment: ignored, or a nuisance and a bother to someone you desperately need to love you. When you grow up feeling inadequate because you don't measure up, you can suffer deep wounds through your entire life.

I wish I had known Jesus then. I wish I had even known to turn to Him for direction and call out to Him for help. But I didn't know. I didn't even recognize His voice when I heard Him speak to me as a very young child. My dad was responsible for me when my mother worked second shift. Often, he would take me with him when he visited his friends. I could hear them laughing inside the house while I waited on the front seat of his old car. One evening, I distinctly remember a voice. "You are going to be all right." It was a masculine voice, and I heard it loudly. Amazingly, I wasn't afraid. Again, I heard the voice. "You are going to be all right." And somehow I was not frightened. I didn't know who it was at the time, but I now realize that was the first time I heard the voice of God. There would be many more times to come.

~ 4 ~

Fathers, do not exasperate your children; instead, bring them up in the training and instruction of the Lord.
—Ephesians 6:4

I didn't realize until I was a grown woman that my dad was an alcoholic and struggled as he tried to numb his life. I don't remember anything personal about my dad, his favorite color or discussions about his youth. He was always very distant and quiet when I was growing up. He must have loved me but could never say the words. One night, I was trying to peel an apple at the kitchen table. He took the knife from me, and said, "My hands are old, and if anyone gets cut, let it be me." Well, that was all I needed to convince me that he loved me.

I have read about fatherless children. Was I a fatherless child?

Lord knows what Papa saw in the war, but it must have caused him great pain. Perhaps he used alcohol to numb the memories of war days. He was discharged medically after being injured from a bullet wound in his leg. That's all that I know. He never talked about the war at any time of his life.

One night, I remember chairs and tables flying around the kitchen and being smashed on the floor. My dad was screaming and my mother was crying. I was so afraid. Mama reassured me the next day, saying, "It's all right, baby. We needed a new table and chairs anyway" (as if Papa had done us a favor). I remember another night when he threw up on the bedroom floor. I didn't know he was drunk at the time. I just remember he was sick, and I was alone and afraid.

When Papa was an old man, he would pat me on the shoulder and cry. Still unable to say the words, I felt that, in his heart, he did love me. He didn't have the tools to show me or the ability to tell me, but I knew that he cared.

Mama said she remembered Papa looking at a picture of himself as a little boy with his sister, and he cried for hours. Mama said his daddy beat him when he was a little boy. I wonder if he beat the tenderness and love so deep down in him that he could not bring it back out again.

One thing he would frequently say was, "Don't get above your raising." He had heard it when he was a little boy growing up. And he didn't get above his "raising." Like his dad, he worked in the cotton mill most of his life. Breaking out of there, he tried his hand at supervising at a local industrial plant, and even got a position in the local post office. He always aspired to more, but could never find his path.

Only when I was older did I begin to see what a funny man my dad truly was! As we both grew older, we had a closer relationship. It was as if he didn't know how to relate to me as a baby or a child, but could talk and laugh with me as an adult.

Sadly, that's exactly what happened to me with my own child. What do we teach our children about who we are? About who they are? How many examples of inadequacy, insecurity, codependency, and searching for love do we pass on to the next generation?

~ 5 ~

One thing God has spoken,
  two things I have heard:
"Power belongs to you, God,
  and with you, Lord, is unfailing love."
                                    —Psalm 62:11-12

I was always chubby as a little girl and can remember Mama taking me to Duke University Hospital in North Carolina to see if they could help me lose weight. I don't remember what they said, and I don't remember any diet changes in the house. I only remember hearing doors slamming down the hall and getting closer and closer. Someone was coming. Suddenly my door opened and a man in a white lab coat and dark black glasses entered the room. He looked at me, spoke to my mama and left, slamming the door to my room.

As a child, I was never thin enough for Mama. When I became a pre-teen, I grew in height and almost naturally lost weight. Mama was so proud.

It was during this time that I developed anorexia and bulimia. I had no control over anything in my life, except that I could control what I would eat. That type of discipline made me feel so good about myself. Hunger pains gave me a sense of power. I could be thin. I would be worthy.

If I did eat something I shouldn't have at my grandmother's, I would have my mother let me out of the car about a mile from the house so I could run home to burn off the calories.

Somewhere in my late teens, I heard about bulimia and gave it a try. You find out as a bulimic that there are not only certain foods or drinks but an order in which you ingest them that makes it easy to throw up. Wow, I actually thought I could "have my cake and eat it too." What a perfect solution for me. I could eat and still control my weight. That disorder remained with me throughout my young adult life.

After several years, it became increasingly difficult to throw up; when I would, my eyes would swell and sometimes get bloodshot. The next morning, I would notice swelling in my hands and fingers. It was one of the physical reasons that I stopped. I knew, somehow, it was going to kill me.

You will pay the price of anorexia and bulimia. The price I pay is a terrible condition called acid reflux and an intolerance to even mild anti-inflammatory medications. The consequences to your physical, emotional, and spiritual health are too great!

When I studied wisdom in the Bible, I learned this great truth: Wisdom watches, listens, and learns. If you are headed down that road of eating disorders—STOP! Get help! Talk to someone! There is a better way for you! One thing I have come to know is that releasing control to God will set you free. There are things in your life that you can do nothing about. Stay focused on what you can change and leave the rest up to Jesus.

~ 6 ~

"I am the LORD your God, who brought you out of Egypt
so that you would no longer be slaves to the Egyptians;
I broke the bars of your yoke and enabled you to walk
with heads held high."
                                                    —Leviticus 26:13

When I was an adult and married, a camp counselor opened my eyes to the fabric of who I had become. My husband and I drove down to Hendersonville, North Carolina so he could find his old boyhood camp, "Pinnacle." We found it, and, on the day of our visit, they were having an open house complete with tours. We met Holly, who greeted us with a warm smile. As we were walking around the site, she began to tell me that the camp's mission (now co-ed) was "to instill worth and empowerment within the children that stayed with them. It's important to prepare them for life and to make them feel good about themselves. To show them 'they can do it.'" My mind stopped to ponder that statement: "to show them that they can do it."

At that moment I realized that I had spent my entire life *trying to show my dad* that *I could do it*. At Girl Scout Camp (somewhere near Greensboro, North Carolina), I remember spending most of my days absolutely miserable, homesick, lost, and lonely. I cried every day (up until a couple of days before my parents came to get me). I would read my mom's letters, and my heart would shrivel. I couldn't enjoy the food, swimming, canoeing, or campfires—at least not until I could see the light at the end of the tunnel and knew I was going home.

Every badge of skill or knowledge I earned, I did for my dad. He had mentioned that I should know about trees. TREES! The Girl Scouts had a badge for trees! I would study trees. And study I did! I knew every tree in that forest, and when they gave me the badge for passing the test, I won that badge for my dad. I did the same thing with swimming and canoeing. I earned these badges for my dad too!

Then the day finally arrived that my parents came to pick me up. I ran to my dad to show him my badges for trees and swimming and canoeing! He couldn't have cared less. He didn't even remember telling me he wanted me to learn about trees. My heart fell. It had not meant one thing to him.

What is enlightening—the insight I finally learned through Holly, all those years later—is that I didn't feel good about MY earning these badges. It was all for him. I had put my entire worth into a man who was unable to acknowledge it.

I have heard Pastor T. D. Jakes talk about "gallon people versus pint people." And I got it; I was a "gallon" girl with a "pint" dad. Not to diminish him. He was a full "pint," and he gave me all that he had. He just didn't have enough to fill a "gallon" girl. I honor, love, and respect him for just who he was. He was on his own spiritual journey—with his own demons and angels. Aren't we all?

The apostle Paul told us to "Forgive as the Lord forgave you" (Colossians 3:13). Forgiveness is the greatest gift of peace that you can give yourself on this earth and perhaps the hardest lesson to master. When you forgive, you release yourself from that prison of anger and resentment.

I have forgiven my parents, and I will continue to forgive them every day for the rest of my life. They did the very best they could with the skills they had. Could they have done better? Sure. Did they make mistakes? Absolutely. But one thing is for sure, they are not to blame for my wrong doings. I am not a victim of their parenting or lack thereof. I didn't come with a "how to" book to guide them. They just struggled to survive and thrive one day at a time. They were clueless, just like I was when trying to parent my own child. Just as we all are as new parents.

~ 7 ~

My mother was so distant that I don't remember her ever really holding me and loving me. She worried about her work. She worried about my weight. She also worried about how I looked and what people thought about me. I felt like I was such a disappointment to her. I know she gave me lots of stuff. I had dresses and toys and playsets that she never had as a little girl.

When I think back, I am my mother in many ways. My mother didn't have "mothering feelings" toward me, and I didn't have them toward my own daughter when she was a little girl. Oh, I wasn't mean or hateful, and I loved her, but I just didn't have the wherewithal to show her. I couldn't sit and read or play games. It was as if there was an empty void within my heart.

When you grow up in an emotionless environment, you don't know any better. I'm here to tell you, you cannot teach what you do not know. I could not feel what I hadn't felt. It is so important for mothers to realize the critical influence they have on their small children. I was just going through life like a breeze, with no idea how my lack of mothering would affect my child. I was so selfishly consumed in myself that I did not realize the emotional detachment that had been passed on to me and was being passed on through me.

By God's grace, my daughter turned out to be an incredible mother. Instead of using me as a role model, she decided to avoid my example at all costs. She cooks with her children, takes them swimming at the pool, reads books with them, and is an active part in their lives. She listens to them and enjoys hearing their stories. If I knew then what I know now—what a difference I would have made in our early relationship. I have often said that it is only by God's grace that my child still loves me. I don't know how it is possible, but we have a strong relationship now as two adult women.

When it comes to my grandchildren, while I love them, I have to be intentional to remember to stop and listen to them. I have to remember my nature and know how critical it is that they know I care, not with money or stuff, but in time spent being with them.

Today, I spend my life encouraging other mothers that it's not too late to turn yourself around in the life of your child. If you don't know your children's favorite colors or inner passions, goals, or aspirations, it is time to stop and make sure that they come first in your life. There will be plenty of alone time for you. Make sure their time is filled with you.

When I look back—at endless hours alone in a car, being afraid of chairs breaking overhead, my mother's emotionally void relationship, and her comparisons to my cousin, and my dad never saying, "I love you"—I understand that life happens in its own way to each of us. How much more bearable my life would have been if I had known Jesus then. I would have looked at each situation through a different set of glasses. I would have known Christ was with me.

What I have come to know is that He suffered along with me and never left me alone. It is critical that you teach your children that God loves them, is with them, and hears their cries. It is critical that you know this about yourself as well.

~ 8 ~

Surely God is my help.
  The Lord is the one who sustains me.
                                    —Psalm 54:4

Now, my parents didn't go to church, but they made sure I went every Sunday. I remember going as a family until I became boy crazy, infatuated with a boy who also attended this particular church. My mother was devastated; he was a second cousin of mine. She was so embarrassed that she and my dad never went back to church again. She threw that up to me years later when I was a young woman; it was *my* fault that they didn't go to church.

How is it that I went to church all my life and don't remember one thing the preacher said? I'll tell you. I was too busy looking at my watch, counting the hymn verses left to sing, and thinking about everything I had to do and could be doing the rest of the day (and about that boy).

It's not supposed to work like that. We're not supposed to just dress up and show up to be counted on the "not guilty" role. "I'm here! I went to church today!" "We never miss a Sunday!" "We are 'churched' up for the week!"

Who was this God they talked about in church? I had no idea. He was someone to celebrate at Christmas in Jesus, the babe in the manger. He was someone who had angels who tended to Him. I knew there was a God, but He sat on a throne somewhere up in heaven, and I was here on earth. He was there when you died—not really here with you as you lived your life everyday. Who was this God? I had no clue.

Our family had a big, expensive-looking, black Bible that we never opened. It had a three-dimensional Jesus on the front. It was always in perfect condition, with no frayed edges, dog-eared pages, or highlighted texts. We didn't read the Bible, and we never prayed together. I never heard stories of knowing God and His loving and caring for me. This doesn't make sense to me, as my mother's father was a Primitive Baptist preacher. He traveled around and preached on Sundays at various churches.

I never learned to pray past "Now I lay me down to sleep. I pray the Lord my soul to keep. If I should die before I wake, I pray the Lord my soul to take." My family never prayed for anything. Or at least not out loud. There were no prayers at mealtime. No thanks and praise. I never knew it mattered.

My mother's mother was an absolute saint. We called her Ma Martin. Short in stature, she had the kindest eyes I have ever seen on anybody. I can still remember watching her wind her long, gray hair up and up and up until it was a perfect little bun on top of her head. I don't know what made her decide, but many years later she cut it short. She always lit up when she would see me coming. I can remember her rocking me as a little girl. I would watch my image sway back and forth in the glass of an old secretary she had in her living room. I remember feeling secure and cared for when I was with her. I was always safe. This was normal.

Ma wore flat, brown loafers in her garden, which she would tend with an old garden hoe. There was an old well covered by a big piece of concrete out back. It would scare me to death when any maintenance required that they take the top off that black hole to nowhere. There was no way I would ever get close to look inside.

There was a giant cherry tree out back, and all the grandkids would climb it and eat cherries until we couldn't hold anymore. There was an old wringer washer in Ma's basement. I would always go down there with her, and she would let me start the clothes through the wringer on the washer. There was a drain in the cold concrete floor. It was damp and cool down there, but the morning sun would come through a small pane of windows going down the steps. Ma had the strangest plants outside her back door. The blossoms looked like little Japanese lanterns and had small cherry-like fruits inside. Old-timey purple, pink, and white phlox lined both sides of her front walkway.

When she passed away, my mother and aunt were crying over her opened casket. I remember having a sense of peace over me. I looked at them, and said, "Why are you crying? She is not gone. You'll see her again." How could I have known that? How did I have peace over the loss of a woman I loved? My mother loved Ma Martin beyond words and, up to the day she passed away herself, she would cry when she thought about her mother coming down the sidewalk to visit her.

Now, when I look back, my grandmother was the very example of Christian living. I don't remember Ma praying or reading the Bible, but she was so tender. Sweet and forgiving. I never ever heard her raise her voice or say an unkind word about anyone. She was the first seed God planted in my heart. God is well known for being with us through life.

> *God has made everything beautiful for its own time. He has planted eternity in the human heart, but even so, people cannot see the whole scope of God's work from beginning to end. (Ecclesiastes 3:11 NLT)*

Isn't that verse the truth? He is in our hearts, yet we can get so caught up in the drama of life that we cannot hear Him—on a page from the Bible or in a sermon on a pew.

I notice that people who don't believe in God get so frustrated with those of us who do. They fight and protest against something they don't even believe. I wonder: If they don't believe it, what is their argument? How can they fight against something that they don't think is here? I'll tell you how. He *is* here; He lives in their hearts too. He is ever present in life and will never stop reminding you who you are and whose you are. There is no escape from the One who "knew you before [He] formed you in your mother's womb" (Jeremiah 1:5 NLT).

Imagine. He knows you. He knows me, and has always been with me. He came alongside me in every trial of life. If I had only known that, my life would have changed.

Watch for His whisper. He will show up in His written Word. The Bible was written for you. There will be moments when your heart will have a joy—lightness—a sense of peace that you cannot describe. I call it the "heart-flip" moment. It's a moment when you don't know how you know but you know that something you saw or read or heard was meant for you. I have come to know that as the calling of the Lord.

After you have suffered a little while, the God of all grace, who has called you to his eternal glory in Christ, will himself restore, confirm, strengthen, and establish you (1 Peter 5:10 ESV).

And, I am living proof.

~ 9 ~

Therefore if you have any encouragement from being united with Christ, if any comfort from his love, if any common sharing in the Spirit, if any tenderness and compassion, then make my joy complete by being like-minded, having the same love, being one in spirit and of one mind.

—Philippians 2:1-2

I am amazed at the people who attend high-school reunions. They must be the folks who felt like they were a part of a "community." I dreaded going to school. Junior high was a lonely place for me. I remember feeling only inferior and worthless.

It was difficult to make friends, but easy to settle for any boy who would pay attention to me. I wouldn't eat in front of anyone, so I went many days with no food. I remember being frightened, and I struggled to have friends. It seemed all the really "cool" people hung around together. The smart ones had their own classes and cliques.

Somehow, I never managed to see the significance of making good grades. I was too busy trying to fit in and get someone to love me. I remember the most popular boy in school asked me for a date! Me? How could he want to be with me? We went riding around town. When he brought me home, I remember sitting on the sofa, and he looked at me and laughed and said, "You are the most naïve girl I have ever met." I smiled, but inside I was dying because I didn't even know what *naïve* meant. I never saw him again. I often wonder if he took me out on a dare of some kind.

I lived like a scared little rabbit. My grades were terrible all through junior high and high school. I got behind early and could never catch up. I remember the finals in a high-school math class. The teacher was passing out the exams, and when he came to me he said out loud, "I don't know why I'm giving you one. You could never pass it." I didn't pass the test, but he promoted me to the next grade anyway. I was just getting further and further behind.

I had only one friend at a time—never several girlfriends. My best friend through high school was so beautiful and popular; and she would come and go in my life, as she needed me. When someone else more popular came along, I got left behind. When she found another "best friend," I was cast aside. I can remember waiting many hours by the phone for my friend to call so we could go out together. On too many nights, that phone never rang. When I think of her now, I feel only rejection.

Here's what I didn't know then. God was always there. He always whispers to someone at just the time you need him or her. I just didn't recognize at the time that He was watching over me. God places people in your life for a reason. Most teachers and principals have no clue how powerful they are in the life of a child, and how God can use them to love someone who doesn't feel loved.

I remember waiting on my mother to pick me up one afternoon from junior high. Standing in the front door, I must have looked like a pitiful sight. Suddenly, out of nowhere, my principal, Mr. Owens, appeared. He put his arm around me, and I began to cry. He said, "It's going to be okay." I never forgot that my entire life. Just when I needed someone, he appeared. I remember another incident when I was crying, and my science teacher, Mrs. Bourne, held me so tenderly. I don't remember what she said, but I remember she had the kindest eyes, and I felt secure.

It was Mrs. Gammons in high school who helped me turn a sharp corner. I didn't qualify to take college transfer courses, so I had to sign up for shorthand and typing. Mrs. Gammons was delightful and always happy to see me. She believed in me when I didn't. She encouraged me when I had no self-confidence. I made straight A's in her classes and began to feel good about myself.

Now, I want to be that someone who encourages others. I want to pay it forward. Like Jesus, who knew a woman had touched the hem of his garment; I want to be aware when someone is reaching out to me.

~ 10 ~

I don't really understand myself, for I want to do what is right, but I don't do it. Instead, I do what I hate.
—Romans 7:15NLT

You don't forget the first love of your life. I don't remember how and when we met, but I remember his clear blue eyes.

He was someone I felt was "above my pay grade." How could someone so handsome and smart look twice at me? I was smitten, and Jeff became the first love of my life. He was with me for most of my high-school days. He respected me and was always there for me.

What happened to me that would make me turn away from him? That he would see the day I was not there for him? How could I forget my first love?

Sometimes we make the worst decisions in our lives and can't explain why we do what we do. Jeff had graduated and gone on to college. I was left alone in high school with one more year to go. Was it because I was alone again that I was vulnerable? I remember exactly when I saw Bob (not his real name). I thought he was so handsome, and I was once again smitten with someone who seemed to be so "cool" and would pay attention to me. I was flattered and intrigued. I couldn't wait to pass him in the hall. One thing led to another, and Bob began to call me at night. We became a couple, and Jeff was left behind.

~ 11 ~

To have a fool for a child brings grief;
   there is no joy for the parent of a godless fool.
                                        —*Proverbs 17:21*

Have you ever looked back and asked yourself, "What was I thinking?" I had been accepted to a college hours away in the Blue Ridge Mountains, and I was scared to death. My bellwether friend had been accepted to go there as well, and I was not looking forward to that. I knew she would never be there for me, and would drop me in a red second if I was in her way. How could I go alone? I wouldn't have any friends. I would be by myself. I would be rejected again and again.

Then Bob proposed to me. I had an idea! I could marry him, and we could keep it a secret. In that way, I could go off to college, and I really wouldn't be alone. I would have an anchor; I would have somebody waiting for me. We did just that. We secretly got a marriage license and found a pastor in a distant town who married us the night of my high-school prom. My mother had no clue. My "best friend" didn't know either.

The instant I said, "I do," I knew I had made a terrible mistake. Weeks passed with me just getting up and going about my usual routine. I remember feeling so empty.

Slowly, I realized this secret marriage was completely insane. We decided to just tell the truth. I will never forget the torment I put on my mother. She was so distraught. She was cutting potatoes with a large butcher knife in the kitchen, and I was afraid she would hurt herself. I ran out of her house. My dad never said a word.

We left for Bob's parents that night. His sister had a singlewide trailer and offered us a bedroom to stay. Here I was, with my parents' hopes and aspirations of me becoming somebody or something, and I was living in a trailer in the country with no car, no education, and no job, with a man I did not love. I thought he was my escape from my home life. But I had gone from one bad situation to another.

Alone and rejected by my parents, I finally got up the nerve and went back to their home. My dad sat in silence while my mother screamed, "My friends asked me if you were pregnant but I told them no; I had washed your dirty underwear just the week before!" Little did she know—and not that she would ever believe it—I was a virgin up to the day I married.

When fall came that first married year of my life, I remember pulling back the curtain in my bedroom. Fall had always been one of my favorite seasons. I loved the color of the leaves and the crispness in the air. But this fall, when I looked at the leaves, I thought about the college in the mountains that I would never attend. All I could think about was what I had given up. All my friends were packing and moving to their college dorms. School and a new life were starting for them, but not for me. That dream was gone, but would never be forgotten.

~ 12 ~

"Before I formed you in the womb, I knew you."

—*Jeremiah 1:5*

Bob and I bought a little four-room house—much like my parents'. We were blessed with dear neighbors who became wonderful friends. Bob got a job with the help of my mother in the cotton mill—much like my dad.

I don't remember, but I think we had been married for about a year when I found out I was pregnant. I was shocked, as I was on birth control. I don't remember being excited. I was never one to understand a "mother's love," so I knew I would never be a good mother to anyone. No "Betty Crocker" for me. Again, my dad said little, and there was a cold distance between my mother and myself during this pregnancy.

One night at about sixteen weeks, I began to spot. The spotting was followed by abdominal cramps. Back then, your husband was not allowed to be with you during labor or miscarriages. Alone, I suffered severe pain in a little bed on the third floor of the local hospital. Suddenly, I felt as if something had passed from me. I called the nurse, who showed me a perfectly formed baby boy. I just looked at him and called my mother. I don't remember a word that she said.

It was so strange that it was only after I was discharged home that I began to feel a terrible loss. I remember being terribly depressed and crying for days until a friend came by with her two kids. They were so noisy and disruptive that we could hardly have a conversation. I thought they would never leave, and when they did—I was over it. I knew this "motherhood" was not for me. The crying stopped, and I went back to work. I never had a desire to have a child again. In fact, when I did get pregnant again, I had an abortion. I couldn't bear the thought of being tied down with a baby.

~ 13 ~

There is a way that appears to be right,
* but in the end it leads to death.*
—Proverbs 16:25

When I read about the hundreds of thousands of abortions that occur every year, I know most of the women are just like me. Please don't judge us. They and I used various methods of birth control and still got pregnant. Caught in a situation of despair, we make a choice that, at the time, seems like the only choice. It's not the only choice. You may make a mistake, but an innocent life is involved.

I remember rationalizing that a child would be better off not being born than being born to me. And even the thought of carrying to term a baby that I didn't want was out of the question. These were dark times in my life—times that are hard to look at, and even think that the woman of my past resembles me.

> *But it was the dark times that Jesus used to make me who I am today. It is those dark times that enable me to hold your hand and talk about another choice. Yes, even another way.*

If you have had an abortion, remember: God loves and forgives you. If you are considering having one, remember this: It seems easy to have an abortion when you are not thinking about a life. But it is a life, and one destined to be. If you became pregnant by someone you do not love, or you feel you could not love this child, remember there are thousands of couples who yearn to love someone and for this someone to love them in return.

The only way I can look back at those times is to know that I have been forgiven. My abortions were all mistakes. Who did I lose that I would have loved? Who did I lose that would have loved me?

~ 14 ~

Therefore encourage one another and build each other up, just as in fact you are doing.
—1 Thessalonians 5:11

My mother had connections, as she had worked loyally in the mills her entire life. She got me a job in the Draper Finishing Mill, where I inspected drapes. That was the saddest place I have ever worked. It just felt desolate. We started work when that lone mill whistle bellowed at 7:00 AM. The whistle would blow again for us to stop for lunch. I remember running out of the mill to my borrowed car to eat. I would do anything to get out of there, even for a few minutes.

I worked right across a large table from another lady. We walked back and forth all day cutting strings from drapes, folding them, and preparing them to be packaged. We were not allowed to talk to each other, so she would whisper to me all day. I would look up and smile; she has no idea that I never heard a word she said. Now there were some men who would smile at me in a way that made my skin crawl. If any of us had to go to the bathroom, we had to raise our hands. And if we went too often, it was written up as an offense. When that old whistle would blow at 3:00 PM, I would run out of there.

In all that despair, I remember a woman who worked on the long line of sewing machines. She sewed the drapes I inspected. Her station was behind me. She had the kindest eyes of any woman I ever met. There was something about her that drew me to her. I heard she was a Christian. I never got the chance to talk to her, but I wanted to sit near her whenever I had a break during the work.

I didn't make the connection of her being there for me as a servant of God when I needed it the most. Jesus talked about being the body of Christ and about "sowing" seeds. Paul talked about sowing seed, and his partner Apollo watering them, but God alone making it grow. It is obvious to me now that this woman was "sowing" more than drapes.

I remember thinking to myself in that dark and lonely place, "I've got to get out of here. And the only way I'm going to do that is to get back in school. If I can get back in school, I could get my self-respect back. What could I take in school? What job could I get that would make me feel good about myself again?" Then, it occurred to me. "My parents will be proud of me again . . . if I could be a nurse."

~ 15 ~

Always be prepared to give an answer to everyone who
asks you to give the reason for the hope that you have.
                                                —1 Peter 3:15

I learned about an open position for a file clerk in the medical department of the mill company. Willing to do anything to get out of that finishing mill, I applied and was accepted for the position. So many lessons and opportunities came with this endeavor.

The department was a place where I learned medical terms and hung around healthcare personnel. The head nurse knew of scholarship opportunities to attend a local nursing school that was offered through the local hospital. I applied and was awarded one of the scholarships. It was a win-win for everybody. The hospital paid for my tuition and I, in turn, would work for them for two years after graduation.

Perhaps the greatest lesson God had for me was "How to be a Christian"—or, rather, Christianity 101.

Where else would I have met Patsy Turner? Patsy was a nurse. Tall, probably in her forties back then, blonde, and slight in demeanor. Quiet. Gentle. Kind. Even though I was so caught up in myself and all the distractions of my world—and even though she was so still (like a little mouse)—you couldn't help but notice her. She stood out in a crowd. It was something about her.

People flocked to her. There was always a stream of people in her office. She always had a gentle smile and a kind word. She was so forgiving and understanding. Non-judging, she never got angry and never got caught up in office politics. She had no part of rumors and no gossip crossed her lips. You could trust her.

I saw her gentle manner—her calming energy— soothe a frightened asthmatic woman one afternoon. I had never seen anything like it. She held her and tended her and soothed her ravaged breath to a gentle whisper. How could anyone be so gentle and so strong?

She treated me like I was somebody important. I had the lowest level job in there, but what I said mattered to Patsy. She would listen to me. You would have thought I was the CEO in her world. She didn't judge me for all the wrong turns I had made in my life. She didn't judge me for the job I did or didn't have. Why, she would even come out of her office and help me file when she didn't have somebody with her.

You know, if you have ever worked in an office or clinic of any kind, that feeling that, if another patient or customer or person showed up at that window, you might scream? Not Patsy. That's why she lived. She looked—she watched—she waited for people to come so she could help them. I think a lot of people faked sick to come to the clinic to just be around her. I know I did.

And, after a year or more of working with her, she was standing in her gentle way with her forehead pressed against the window—looking out across the parking in anticipation of another patient. I asked her "What is it about you that you are so different? How is it you never get mad? And she told me about her love of Jesus Christ and how He ruled her world and how she was His servant. I didn't understand exactly all she was saying, but I never forgot it. And I know this: Because of a timid, quiet woman in Draper, North Carolina, I started going to Sunday school to meet a God I did not know.

What I came to know is that Patsy Turner was anointed. Patsy was a fisher of men, a gardener—watering the seed that God planted in your heart.

What is it about you? Do you stand out in a crowd? Are you ready with an answer when someone asks you, "How is it that you are different than everybody else?"

Patsy moved away and out of my life, but her mission was done in that medical clinic—that season of her life. God had others He needed her to seed for Him. I lost touch with Patsy Turner. But when we are at the Holy gate ... the Lord's going to look at Patsy Turner and say, "Well done, my good and faithful servant. Now, who did you bring with you?" And, when she turns around, she's going to be looking at me.

Who will be standing behind you?

Step back now and look at what God has and is doing in your life and the lives of so many more. I heard Bishop T.

D. Jakes say that God always has somebody there to bless you. No matter where you are in your life, no matter what kind of situation you're in, He will bring up, call out, and anoint someone to bless you.

Bishop Jakes also reminds me that some people—with the job they have and the power, position, and influence they hold—God gave it to them so that there would be somebody on the inside who loved God and loved His people; so in a time of trouble, and when they get themselves into trouble, there would be somebody there to bless them.

Years later, in the same medical department, He would send me another person to teach me a different kind of lesson. I was several years older but still a hot mess, searching for love in all the wrong places. But God always takes something bad in your life and can turn it to the glory of His kingdom.

~ 16 ~

"If you hold to my teaching, you are really my disciples.
Then you will know the truth, and the truth will set you free."
—John 8:31-32

My first marriage lasted only five years. Shamefully, I have to say, with my insecurities and the empty hole in my life, I left my first husband for the love of another man. It was wrong from the beginning. Affairs rarely end well. Somebody always gets hurt along the way. And that somebody is often you.

People often ask me what God thinks about divorce. It's pretty clear that God doesn't want us to divorce. Jesus mentions marriage and divorce several times. When you marry, the two of you become one and "what God has joined together, let no one separate" (Matthew 19:6). He also says that if you do divorce and marry someone else, the two of you commit adultery (see Mark 10:4-12).

I don't know much, but I know this: I have been married three times, and I'm going to heaven too. God never chose those first two men in my life for me. I had all the red flags of "Don't do it," but I did it anyway. I reaped what I sowed.

You've got those red flags too! I call it a "check in your spirit." Be careful if you get a "check in your spirit," and something just doesn't feel right or you are uncomfortable when he said what he did to you. Pay attention! Don't brush it off.

It may be that you are living in denial so you don't have to look at the truth. Maybe you are marrying for all the wrong reasons, like security, money, or influence. Or perhaps you think this person will fill your empty hole of loneliness.

Think again. If in doubt—any doubt at all—don't do it. Get into God's Word. Ask Him to guide you in this situation. Look boldly at your situation, and don't be afraid to face the truth.

It is far better to be alone than with someone who does not love you. And there is a difference in being alone and being lonely. Know the difference before you make any decisions. Ask yourself, "Why am I so miserable alone? Is this sadness or fear that I am feeling? Do I like who I am? Can I enjoy the stillness? Can silence become a friend and not an enemy?" These are the questions you must answer to help you understand why you would choose to be with someone who shoots off warning bells and raises red flags for you.

The wonderful man who is now my husband works out of town, so I am alone most of the time. I am alone, but I am not lonely. I am free to do what I want and need to do with no guilt or other obligations. I love being with the Lord throughout the day. I love what He gives me in sunrises, rain showers, and birds of all colors and sizes. I love having a purpose in life working for Jesus. I love getting up, and I love going to bed. None of these things meant anything to me until I became who Jesus says that I am.

Who does He say that you are?

~ 17 ~

I planted the seed, Apollos watered it, but God has been making it grow. So neither the one who plants nor the one who waters is anything, but only God, who makes things grow. The one who plants and the one who waters have one purpose, and they will each be rewarded according to their own labor. For we are co-workers in God's service; you are God's field, God's building.
—1 Corinthians 3:6-9

There is something about turning forty years old that makes a person stop and think, "What was I thinking, and what on earth am I doing here?" I was in my second marriage when I turned forty, and that is exactly the question I began to ask myself. I was in a loveless marriage to a man (I'll call him Jim), who could not fully commit to me emotionally or physically. I lived denying any wrong he could do for the sake of not being alone. After all, he didn't beat me. He never laid a hand on me. He just needed far more than I or any woman could bring him. He could not make a commitment to anyone.

I even rationalized that, if Jim could not meet my needs as a woman, then I should be able to see other men. We would still stay married, but I would just run around on the side. And run around, I did.

At this time, I worked with a woman who taught me the next lesson in how to be a Christian (or how not to be). I'll call her *Bonnie* (not her real name). A "Christian" woman, Bonnie never missed a day's church. She was there when the doors opened and could quote more scripture than the town priest. With all her honesty and piety, we would tiptoe around Bonnie and never curse or do anything out of the way to offend her. She was such an example for me.

As usual, what is done in dark comes out into the light, and what I was doing in secret got out in public. I came into work the following day, and Bonnie turned her back, tipped her nose up in the air, and never spoke to me again. She treated me like I was something vile and dirty. Broken already, I needed the love of a Savior.

I know there is someone out there who has been through the same thing. Let me tell you how God works it to your good. I learned how to treat people. I learned early on how it feels to be judged for something you already know is wrong, and I learned to meet people where they are and love them anyway. I learned to never cast the first stone.

You have no clue of the power and influence you have in the lives of young women you will meet.

Grab those young women by the shoulders because you love them, and say, "Wait—stop! Not on my watch! I love you and God loves you and I'm not going to let you do this."

We all have the opportunity at any age and in any circumstance to bring the kingdom of heaven near to someone. To show someone He lives in you. It doesn't matter what position God has you in—you have the opportunity—through the power of Jesus Christ, to influence someone's life.

Throughout my turbulent, fleshly life, God was always with me. He always whispered to me, came along beside me, and planted seeds along the way. There are always those people he places in your life at just the right moment. You may not realize it at the time, but I can look back and see His presence through my entire life. You too will be able to look back and find them.

I live to be a seed of hope in someone's life. You have that power within you, by the grace of Jesus Christ, to make a difference in the lives of people you meet. You may go through your whole life and never realize the purpose God has given you, but don't ever give up.

And, just like my first Christian mentor, Patsy Turner, when, at heavens gate, God wants to know whose life you touched on earth—turn around—there may be thousands of people standing behind you, and you had no clue. You have a ripple effect.

~ 18 ~

Jesus straightened up and asked [the adulterous woman], "Woman, where are they? Has no one condemned you?"

"No one, sir," She said.

"Then neither do I condemn you," Jesus declared. "Go now go and leave your life of sin."

—John 8:10-11

When you hear of a woman having affairs, please know she is vulnerable, and be kind to her. There is a reason for her vulnerability. Perhaps like the woman Jesus met at the well, she feels alone, even afraid.

No woman secure in herself would get involved with a man that was not her own or turn to alcohol to numb her pain. No woman dreams as a little girl of becoming an adulteress or an alcoholic. Perhaps she is living a life similar to mine, with a driving need to be worthy, recognized, and important to someone.

While I was in a loveless marriage that was a mistake from the beginning, that was no excuse for my actions. I was absolutely no different than a prostitute. It's just that I was not getting paid; I was giving it away. How could I think that having affairs could heal my sick relationship?

Stop giving yourself away. Your womanhood is fragile, delicate, valuable—a gift from God—not to be wasted, not to be given away, not to be used, not to be had, not to be cast aside—but to be honored; a fine jewel, a precious commodity, to be cherished and saved for the man God has chosen for you. You are worthy to be waited for!

I talk with so many women today who have no clue who they really are. They know what other people say, but it has never occurred to them who Christ says that they are. Who are you? What does Christ say about who you are? Not what and whom other people say you are—not what your mama said, your co-workers, your neighbors, your friends, your husband, not that boyfriend—but who Christ says that you are.

Far too many women worry about what other people say. They take it on and wear it like a burden. I've heard too many stories. "Well," they say, "I don't love my son. I act like I don't care. I run around with my neighbor." And there's no truth in it! Stand in your truth. You have an audience of One!

God is the authority of who you are. Only Christ defines you—God the Father created you, and He creates only what He loves. You were created—with great love, great spirit, great gifts and passions, and a desire to make a difference—to be His hands and feet in this world.

You've been gifted with many talents and passions in your heart. Realize that God has blessed you to fulfill His purpose for you in this life! It is critical to know who you are in Jesus. Knowing Him and having a relationship with him is paramount in making right choices.

When I had affairs in the past, I had no clue who Jesus was. I knew God was up in heaven, and I was here on earth—but a relationship? What does that look like? I was trying to find someone to love me, never knowing that there was the One within me who loved me compassionately. I never knew this "Jesus," who would guide me and teach me the ways of the Father.

The Bible tells us that love does a neighbor no harm (Romans 13:10), and that love does not dishonor others and is not self-seeking. Love always protects, trusts, and hopes (1 Corinthians 13). None of this is true in an affair. People get hurt and embarrassed. Children are torn apart. Spouses struggle to trust again. There is no peace within an affair. It is always searching and seeking to self-fulfill in emotion. If you find yourself being drawn to someone who does not belong to you, ask Jesus to intervene.

Keep nothing from Jesus. He already knows your thoughts and feelings. He is your rock. He is your fortress. You are not alone. You have never been alone.

Be kind to women seeking love in all the wrong places. I've been one of those women. Be loving toward their hearts, and, if given a chance, tell them about your love of Jesus. The Holy Spirit will prompt you when to say something. Be very tender with your words. I remember the Apostle Paul writing about how some people are able to eat meat but others need milk, because they are just not ready to hear the full revelations of God's Word. Give them the milk of God in your compassion and understanding. Tell them tenderly how you love Jesus and how His love set you free. They already feel trapped; don't add to it.

When caught in a situation that you already know is wrong, it can make you a prisoner of shame. You can be set free of that disgrace. Jesus Christ died for her sins, your sins, and mine. We all have been forgiven. Our slates are wiped clean.

~ 19 ~

*Praise the L*ORD*, my soul,*
and forget not all his benefits—
who forgives all your sins
and heals all your diseases
who redeems your life from the pit
and crowns you with love and compassion.
—Psalm 103:2-4

I finally did have a child, a daughter. I'm not sure how and why my only child loves me. I gave her every reason to hate me and never trust me again. I was not there when she was little. Even while in the house, I was not at home.

I have never been someone who knows what to do with babies and small children. I don't seem to possess that internal "mothering love" that I envy in so many women.

That doesn't mean I don't love my one and only child. I have always loved her with all my heart. So what is wrong with me? When she was ten days old, I cried over her while lying on the floor beside her. I felt so sad that she had me for a mother. I was completely inadequate.

My mother hired a housekeeper for me when I brought my daughter home. I would ask Nannie, "What do I do with her?" And, she would smile a big, broad smile, and say, "Well you just put her toys in her crib, and pick her up and walk her outside." I had no natural mothering instincts at all.

My distance and disconnect seems to be only with babies and small children, because, as my child grew, so did my relationship with her. And when I look back, this is exactly what happened with my dad and me. He was completely removed from me as a child, but as a grown woman, I had a much closer relationship with him.

It is only by God's grace that my child forgives me. I cared about her deeply; when she was dating, I would cry and wring my hands if she were ever late coming home. Rationalizing that so many people loved her; she really would never miss me. She had grandparents on both sides, her father, and every material possession you could imagine. But what she needed most was to know and feel the love of her mother. Family is great, fathers are invaluable, but no one and nothing takes the place of your mother.

I went through a phase of such regret and remorse after my daughter was grown that I overcompensated in my relationship with her. I could not do enough, be enough, or buy enough for her. One day, after I had tried so hard and was unable to get her on the phone, it dawned on me: I cannot make this child happy. I cannot rescue, save, or fix her. I can only love her and pray for her.

That very day I prayed to Jesus, "Lord, she's yours. I am turning her over to your care. I will always be there for her and love her, but I am going to stop beating myself up and get on with your purpose for me in this life." I had a sense of peace come over me, and I stopped pestering, bothering, buying, and calling all the time.

God in His great mercy has been with both of us. I know He watches over her and her family. After all, she is His child too. I stand on His Word, because He has helped me through the guilt and pain of something that I cannot go back and change. I can only go forward and open my heart to other women who are living in the guilt of their past. We all did the best we could with the tools we had to use, and most important, we are forgiven.

~ 20 ~

*Be merciful to me, O L*ORD*, for I am in distress;*
my eyes grow weak with sorrow,
my soul and body with grief.
—Psalm 31:9

You can get caught up into some stories that are not yours to tell. A mother's worst nightmare is the terror of discovering her baby girl was violated as a young child. Innocent and new to the world, these babies are at the mercy of people they were told to trust.

Young children are learning to trust in their early days; when that trust is so severely violated in such a perverted and unnatural manner, they can suffer for the rest of their lives.

Their mamas suffer too. This stabbing leaves a deep wound; the news leaves a festering, twisted path of guilt and shame. How could this happen on my watch? How is it that I also trusted this predator?

Were there signs? How did I miss them? Abuse such as this would be the furthest thing from any mother's imagination.

Be aware—it could happen to you and your baby. It is likely your child knows and trusts the abuser, so never, ever let your guard down around anyone who is in close contact with your child.

Watch for any signs of fear and insecurity. They can look like nightmares, fear of the dark, depression, loss of interest in activities, seclusion, inability to trust, or nervous habits such as nail biting or compulsive behaviors.

It is tough but critical that you forgive yourself. A television commentator once said, "The mother always knows." But I am here to tell you—that is not true. Most mothers are blindsided and paralyzed with fear, not only with the agony of this breech of innocence but also the desperation of watching their children try to deal with, suffer through, and heal these wounds in their hearts.

Our only hope is in knowing that we have a God who is the divine healer of all wounds. I pray that God continues to heal our children, and that they recognize their complete innocence in such a horrendous time in their lives.

A Mother's Prayer

"Lord, we pray for our children who were so brutally injured in such a tender time of emotional development in their lives. Bring them to you, Lord so that they know how very special they are and how much you love them. Heal them, Lord, and heal the mothers too. Remove their pain of the past. Take away any guilt that they carry. We did not know, Lord. You alone know that is our truth. Father, the hardest part is dealing with the one who committed this terrible sin. You'll have to help us forgive them. There are some things we cannot do alone. But, you, O Lord, can do all things. In you, we place our trust. In Jesus Name, Amen. So be it."

~ 21 ~

I can do all things through [Christ] who strengthens me.
—Philippians 4:13 ESV

I was so insecure I could not bear the thought of leaving Jim, my daughter's father. That led to my decision to try a pleasant separation while remaining friends. Obviously, he wasn't happy in the marriage either. If we could remain close friends, then I wouldn't be alone. I could count on him to be there for me in any situation. We agreed to a separation. I began to purchase household items that I thought he would need and enjoy.

I was in the middle of telling one of my friends about my shopping for Jim when she stopped me in my tracks. "That's it." she said. "I've had enough. You have got to open your eyes and see for yourself what is going on." I found out truths that night about my husband that I could not believe.

This man was supposed to be my best friend. How could he do these things with other women and yet not be there for me? How could he betray me and come home like nothing was wrong?

I was devastated. I think God gives us a state of shock to protect us from harm. We literally become frozen in time and incapable of making any decisions or judgments. I don't remember the ride home from her house. I remember confronting my husband and his crying.

I vaguely remember that my daughter was home. She later told me that she heard accusations and chose to run from them. Like me, she couldn't bear to hear the truth.

I asked Jim to leave, never thinking he would. But, he left; He walked right out that door. I later found out that he was seeing another woman: a beautiful young woman. One of my co-workers had seen them together in her car at the back of a fast food restaurant in the middle of a work day.

Other people came out of the woodwork. "I saw him here." "I saw him there." These people never said a word to me all those years. It's funny how they come out after having known all along. I spent months worrying about what other people were saying. Thank goodness I had a true friend who told me in private out of love and concern for me.

Isn't it strange how we can deny our own sins and at the same time be outraged and unforgiving of the sins of others? It's as if we protect ourselves by living in denial of the truth. I lived in denial of my loveless marriage and my husband's rumored behavior! Because I couldn't face the fact that our marriage was dysfunctional, I justified my affairs as appropriate and acceptable. What hypocrisy! While devastated at his betrayal, I was guilty of the same betrayal!

The next weeks and months are a blur. I remember agreeing to give our marriage another chance. I didn't want to go to my grave not having tried one more time, and yet, in my spirit, I knew it was wrong. That second chance didn't last a week. The entire scam of a marriage became repulsive to me.

My parents are from the school of "you stay with the job you have and the man you marry, no matter what happens." Needless to say, my parents were furious that I was a separated woman. My dad even said to me, "Maybe if you wore a nice nightgown, he would come around." I don't think they ever believed Jim did anything wrong; somehow all the problems were mine alone to bear.

I often wonder about all those years of doubt and emptiness. All that time wasted with endless searching for love and worth. Where was God during those times? If He was with me, how is it I didn't hear Him?

This culture we live in tries to get you to believe you are invincible and can do everything by yourself. You are taught to think that, if you need help, somehow you are weak and worthless. There is no truth to this at all. You cannot do this alone. You must be led by God in such a world of grief, mistrust, and dysfunction. Only with His help can you have true peace and joy.

I know now that those "checks in my spirit" were Him calling me. It was God's voice saying, "Pay attention. Warning. Danger ahead." I know now He was whispering, "Come to me. I am here for you." Looking back, I know that to be true, but when you don't know Jesus, you just run right by those warning signs and try to figure things out for yourself. You don't ever have to go it alone again.

I cannot tell you what peace I have today knowing that Christ has not only forgiven me but has also forgiven Jim for our betrayals of each other. There is such joy knowing that no matter what you have done, your pardon was completed at the cross. As Jesus said, "Go, and sin no more" (John 8:11KJV).

~ 22 ~

I sought the L<small>ORD</small>, and he answered me;
*   he delivered me from all my fears.*
Those who look to Him are radiant;
*   their faces are never covered with shame.*
This poor man called, and the L<small>ORD</small> heard him;
*   he saved him out of all his troubles.*
The angel of the L<small>ORD</small> encamps around those who fear him,
*   and he delivers them.*
—Psalm 34:4-7

If I had known Jesus, my recovery time from separation and divorce would have been much shorter. But, when you don't now Jesus, you don't know where or how to look for Him.

In the middle of the night after Jim left, I remember praying to God to help me. I said, "Lord, I know you have these guardian angels. And, if that is true, send me mine tonight. And, if it's ok with you, send me two."

Angels began to show up in my life. My hairdresser gave me a picture of a woman she said reminded her of me; and behind this woman was an angel. Out of the clear blue, my daughter, having no clue about my prayer, gave me a book on angels.

Every night I would remind God to send me my angels. One particular night, I was feeling a little more secure and prayed "Lord, thank you for my angels; if there is a woman out there who is suffering like I have suffered, it's ok with me if you lend her one of my angels. But, please don't send both. Leave one for me."

I learned through pain and despair that getting outside of yourself and helping someone else will help you heal. One day, I heard the words: "March of Dimes." I thought: March of Dimes? What is this about, and where did that thought come from?

I found out that the March of Dimes was having a fundraiser in Greensboro, North Carolina. The fundraiser was held on a cold, rainy, dreary day. I didn't want to go, but I didn't want to stay home either. Something just kept tugging at me to go. Sometimes you have to just get your feet moving and do the next right thing. I was assigned to the "pick up the ducks" booth, where children came and picked up plastic ducks to see if they had won a prize marked on the underside. I felt numb. I didn't know anybody. I was just trying to do something good. I don't remember the children or the adults. I only remember the yellow plastic ducks going around and around in a swirling stream of water.

It was a long, cold drive home. I pulled in the driveway, and went into an empty house. I remember building a fire in the fireplace. After taking a long, warm bath, I curled up on the sofa with a soft blanket and, for the first time, I felt this deep contentment. To this day, the crackling of wood and the warmth of flickering flames bring a certain peace in my heart.

That feeling of peace and contentment didn't last long—maybe not even a minute—but when I look back, it was a sign of healing. I was on the road to recovery.

Recovery sometimes comes in short bursts and snaps throughout your life. You may not even recognize that you are healing until months or years have passed by. Only then can you look back and see that God was always with you. He will keep His promise to guide and protect you. He will send His angels to whisper to you in the darkest nights. Open your eyes and ears to hear the glory of the Lord.

~ 23 ~

There is a time for everything,
and a season for every activity under the heavens.
—Ecclesiastes 3:1

I remember when Jim left; I didn't know what to do with myself. I lamented about him day and night to all my friends. It is amazing how your friendships with other women deepen when you are alone. They were there all along. I just didn't make time to cultivate them past an occasional outing.

I remember Debbie, one of my best friends to this day, telling me that divorce was "like a long dark tunnel. There is a light at the end of the tunnel. Now, you have got to go through the tunnel. But your friends who have been through it; we have flashlights, and we are going to shine the light on your path so you don't stumble up and fall the way we did." She was such a light of Christ in my life. I have shared her great wisdom hundreds of times with women going through the tunnel.

Debbie also stopped me in my tracks. I was crying over Jim's bad behavior. She looked at me and said, "Stop. I'm tired of hearing about him. I know all about what he did. I want to hear about you." That set me back on my heels because I didn't know what to say. I had no idea who I was. I knew what "we" liked, but I didn't know what "I" liked. I knew the colors "we" liked, but couldn't tell you "my" favorite color. I remember going to pick out Christmas cards and not knowing what I liked or what represented who I was. I stood, picking up every box in the store, and I could not decide which cards represented what I wanted to say.

Everybody has a purpose in this life. Even Judas Iscariot lived his purpose on this earth by betraying Jesus. My ex-husband lived his purpose by leaving me.

If he had not left me, I may have never become who I am today. And, by becoming Pat, I have become secure in who I am and not who anyone else says that I am.

I developed deep relationships with my girlfriends. I was driven to obtain a Master's Degree in Nursing. I started enjoying culinary gourmet foods—often dining alone in wonderful restaurants in nearby cities. I began to travel by myself to fabulous resorts and enjoyed their spas and front porch rocking chairs. I had always loved to run, but now I was able to take it to a new level, running up to five miles a day followed by forty minutes in the local gym. Life was good. I was content and optimistic about life.

So have I forgiven Jim and moved on with my life? You bet, and I give thanks to God for his coming into my life and abruptly leaving. He was there for a season of awakening. If I was still in that loveless relationship, I might have taken forever to get on the spiritual journey of finding Jesus. Without that experience, I might still be trapped in a place of uncertainty and self-destruction.

~ 24 ~

Many are the plans in a person's heart,
but it is the LORD's purpose that prevails.
—Proverbs 19:21

I tried dating, but, believe me, it is not for the faint of heart. Red flag: There may be a reason a man is still single. After several miserable attempts, I came to know that the last thing I needed in my life was a man. I was doing pretty well by myself.

Then, one Thanksgiving . . . things changed.

I was planning to work at the soup kitchen in a neighboring town, when the phone rang. It was dear friends inviting me to Thanksgiving brunch! They lived about two hours away in a small town at the foot of the Blue Ridge Mountains. This is a couple I always adored, so without hesitation, I said yes. When I was about five minutes from their home, Maria called, "We can't wait for you to get here and, oh, by the way, we have invited a gentleman we want you to meet."

Oh brother, I thought. Just what I need . . . a blind date. I was not happy and wished I had gone to the soup kitchen. I found out later, this gentleman was Trip Farrell. Maria had also called him when he was about five minutes from her house. Trip was divorced and living in the same town as my friends. He was also finished with dating women and not happy about this "date." We both came into Thanksgiving brunch mad.

After glaring at each other through lunch, Trip and I began to talk. What was appealing to me about him was the fact that he didn't "need" me. He was a man of his own, secure in who he was and in his medical practice. Later on, he would tell me the same thing about me. The fact that I was secure and independent was appealing to him.

When you get to the point that you like yourself and are happy with whom you are, then you are ready for a relationship with someone else. We realized we both loved school, medicine, the mountains, and running!

When he asked me if he could call me in the future, I remember saying, "Yes, but wait until after December. I'm working on my thesis for school." He didn't wait, but I was happy to hear his voice on the telephone! We started a long-distance relationship that ended up with him proposing and me saying yes.

Trip and I tried living in the small town where we met, but it was a horrible experience. Here we were, newly married and living in the unfriendliest environment that I have ever experienced. It was a place that, if you were not born there, you didn't belong there.

I tried to make friends at the hospital and with the other physicians' wives. I joined the Art Association and tried to get active in their fundraisers. Surely, I thought, the church would be a place I could find a home. We tried several churches, but most people just stared at us for a moment and then turned back around. I don't even think the pastor at the last church we attended liked people. I lived there for one year, and our only friends were our accountant and the pathologist at the hospital and his wife. It was a lonely place.

When a hospital representative from my hometown called to ask us to join their team, we were thrilled. The moving trucks came, and off we went. I was back where I started. However, that didn't go so well either. Jesus said a prophet in his own town has no merit. Neither does a divorced woman returning with a whole new life. Here I was, with the most wonderful man and secure marriage, but I was never accepted back into the community. And, until Trip made his own way, he wasn't accepted either. He was just Pat Priddy's husband. It didn't take long for him to stand on his own without me.

It was nice being close to my home and my parents. Little did I know how short-lived that time would be.

~ 25 ~

They found rich, good pasture, and the land was spacious, peaceful and quiet.

—1 Chronicles 4:40

God's call can be sudden and profound or like a gentle whisper in your heart. Often it is step-by-step as He slowly draws you closer to His presence and great love. He is always with you, and will never do anything to turn you away from His love. We do that by ourselves.

My husband is a wonderful physician. He loves people and follows a strict standard of care in medicine. I was not surprised when a physician recruiter began to contact him about a position, but I was surprised that it was in New Mexico. "New Mexico? What on earth is in New Mexico?"

Trip was excited about the prospect of filling the need for an Ear-Nose-Throat physician in an area that was lacking in the specialty. My response was, "Well, I don't guess it would hurt to go see the area and talk with the hospital administration."

The hospital flew us into Midland, Texas, in the middle of the night. (I was told later on that there was a reason for us to arrive after dark.) We drove into New Mexico and checked in to a Holiday Inn. I don't remember there being too many options on where to stay. The next morning, I opened up the curtains, and I was looking out at nothing—and nothing was looking back. Flat—nine miles to the horizon. All I saw was lots of sand and few trees. No wonder they brought us in during the night. It was so open. I could see forever; I was used to seeing trees and water!

My rational brain kept saying, "This isn't going to work for me." But there was a little voice deep inside of me that just kept whispering, "Do it. Just do it." I remember thinking, "This makes no sense at all. My mind says no, but my heart keeps saying yes." I followed my heart, and came to know that it was God's Spirit in me that was whispering.

New Mexico is truly the land of the enchanted. The skies seemed enormous! And the colors of the sunsets and sunrises are more vibrant than I had ever experienced before. There was a quietness in the desert plains that I had not experienced in the bustle of small towns on the East Coast.

The first year or two while I was there, I enjoyed my new house, new language, new weather patterns, food, and friends. But about my third year in New Mexico, I began to ask, "Lord, what am I doing in the desert?"

Several weeks later, a life coach came on the television. I remember sitting in my kitchen and being mesmerized by what she was saying. When she said she helped women with low self-esteem, my heart flipped. I stood up slowly and thought, "I qualify for that, because I never had any self-esteem." It is so true that we teach what we need to know.

I signed up with "Coach U" and, in the desert of my life, I became a life coach. I started coaching women in Family Drug Court. They were all types of women. They were all ages, races, and socioeconomic status. They were women coming out of rehab, trying to make a life, and they changed my life. They taught me how mean we are to one another and how judgmental we can be. They taught me that, in the blink of an eye, you can lose everything you have, and that we are all just women.

God can take you to the desert of your life and put your feet on the journey of finding your purpose in life. Sometimes, He calls you to go down the desert road, but it will not be in vain. Your travels will teach you more of who you are and whose you are in Him.

~ 26 ~

As he neared Damascus on his journey, suddenly a light from heaven flashed around him. He fell to the ground and heard a voice say to him, "Saul, Saul, why do you persecute me?"

"Who are you Lord?" Saul asked.

"I am Jesus, whom you are persecuting," he replied. "Now get up and go into the city, and you will be told what you must do."

—Acts 9:3-6

I never drank as a teenager or young adult. I never had the desire to drink. When everyone else was having frozen lime daiquiris or just cold beer, I was perfectly happy with a soft drink.

One of my friends from high school had opened up a wine and cheese shop in my hometown. After Jim left, I began to shop in her gourmet food section. She invited me to dinner in Greensboro. I was so depressed and dejected, I almost didn't go, but I made myself get dressed and get out of the house.

I met Kim at the Undercurrent Restaurant on Elm Street, and she introduced me to ... the chardonnay. "It's rich and buttery," she said, "and has wonderful vanilla undertones." "Really? It tastes bitter to me," I thought under my breath as I tried to swirl the wine, almost spilling it, and holding it on my tongue to determine the flavors. "This stuff is terrible." But I "paired it with my food" and thought I looked so debonair and polished.

Well, it may have tasted terrible, but I got a happy "buzz." I remember almost laughing gleefully on the way home. And, most important, for the first time in a long time, I didn't mind going to an empty house. I didn't mind Jim not being there. I was ok being alone. Oh, this chardonnay was quite a new friend.

Several days passed, but I didn't forget the new happiness I had discovered. I began to rationalize: "It's ok, because everybody drinks wine with their meals"; "lots of folks have a glass of wine to 'wind down' after work." After all, "It's five o'clock somewhere!" I would just be part of the crowd. I'd fit right in with today's culture.

I remember going by Kim's shop and buying my first bottle of wine. It would be the first of many bottles. The chardonnay became my new friend in the lonely afternoons at home. I clearly remember the exact moment when I knew I was addicted. I had opened my refrigerator, leaned in, and put my hand on that cold bottle in the door when I knew. "You're becoming addicted—red flag!" And, I didn't listen. I hardly hesitated except to acknowledge what I heard and felt as I poured that pale yellow anesthesia into a tall-stemmed glass.

At first, I would just have a glass when I was home—on the weekends. Then that progressed to a couple of glasses. My palate expanded as I exposed myself to red wine. Oh, now that was a treat. That little explosion has undertones of chocolate and cherries! Soon it was champagne. The fancier the drink, the more sophisticated I would feel. Don't fool yourself.

How bad can that be for you? It can be bad. Very bad. I was on the path to know the lure of addiction for the next six years.

When I met my Trip, I was at the point of having a glass or two on Friday or Saturday night. But my body craved more. Even though my life had changed for the best and I had met a man who loved me, I was addicted to alcohol. Here I was in New Mexico, secretly searching "AA" on the web and starting to wonder if even God could or would help me.

I continued my alcohol addiction with wine and champagne. I began to want to drink during the week, but I knew Trip would know the truth about me. He had married an alcoholic. I began to sneak and drink—just a glass or two—during the week before he came home. What was wrong with me that I could not stop? I could not live without a drink. What was life without a drink? The very thought of not having wine was depressing to me.

Drinking and enjoying alcohol was so wonderful . . . what would life be without it? What would I look forward to? To lose my wine would be like losing my best friend. What would I do? How would I cope?

And, yet, my life *was* wonderful. I had a man who absolutely adored me and always made me feel I was enough! We had a wonderful life; why couldn't I give this alcohol up? I had been able to give up cigarettes,

Valium, even addictive toxic relationships, but this demon kept rearing his ugly head.

I began to pray. I prayed and asked God to please help me. I journaled. I exercised. I ate the right foods. I still could not stop. I went to church. Took vitamins. Meditated. Read everything I could read about addiction. And I was powerless to stop.

I never stopped turning to God for help, but I wasn't sure why He wouldn't help me. "Lord," I prayed, "I surrender. Please take this from me. I cannot do this by myself. This battle is yours, and only You can fight and win this battle for me."

A miracle happened at my kitchen table in Hobbs, New Mexico. I was not a Bible reader at the time and did not know what the scriptures say about turning to God, and how He shows Himself to us. I did not know about the references to "flashes of lightning." But at that kitchen table I saw and felt a flash of lightning: A brief flash—noiseless—but bright and blinding. And, at that moment, I heard in my heart (and those of you who have heard God speak know exactly what I am saying), "If life is good and joyful, why do you need a buzz?"

And, at that moment in my life, my entire life changed. I sat there mesmerized. Setting still and soaking in what just happened, I realized I didn't need a buzz. My husband was wonderful. I had a beautiful home and a healthy child. Life was a buzz. Life was joyful. I didn't need to drink to feel the goodness of what was all around me.

My cravings stopped that day. I never drank again. God completely took that desire for alcohol away from me. I don't know why it took so long. Perhaps God was watching me to see if I would indeed completely surrender myself. Could it be that He wanted me to experience addiction at its fullness so that now I can help others? Not only can I say, "I understand," but I can truly witness to the power and might of our Creator and what He is capable of doing.

In a flash of light, your entire life can change. Don't you ever give up hope. Don't you ever give up on God. He will never give up on you.

~ 27 ~

All Scripture is God-breathed and is useful for teaching,
rebuking, correcting and training in righteousness, so
that the servant of God may be thoroughly equipped
for every good work.
—2 Timothy 3:16-17

There is no doubt that the Lord called me to New Mexico. It was there that I witnessed the miracle of alcohol being removed from my life. It was in New Mexico that I started to pray more often and even attended a Bible study. Beth Moore's study of the book of Daniel absolutely gave me the "heart-flip" moment and much to ponder during the week. It was also good to surround myself with other women who were searching for the Lord.

But it was in my pastor's Bible study that a particular verse resonated so profoundly with me, I couldn't let it go for weeks. It still comes to my heart to this day. We were studying the book of John, and Jesus was speaking to His disciples. When the pastor read the verse "I will ask the Father, and he will give you another [Counselor] to be with you forever" (John 14:16), I remember leaning inward, wanting to know more about this Counselor. A Counselor for me? My own protector and guide?

It was with that verse that I knew God had spoken to me. And, once you have tasted the Word of God, you cannot get enough. I wanted to know more about God and what He had to say to me.

I was determined to have that awareness again. I wanted God to reconnect with me. I would sit and read the Bible, but just couldn't understand the passages. I would read it, and it would "fall flat" on the page. "I don't understand this Lord! These stories don't make sense to me. They were written too long ago to be relevant to people today. The cultures are just too different." Sound familiar? But I never gave up.

Every night I would pick up the Bible and say to myself, "Well, I remember how I felt, and I know you're supposed to read it, so I'm going to try it again." One night, I opened the Bible to the very verse I needed to read: "For the eyes of the Lᴏʀᴅ range throughout the earth to strengthen those whose hearts are fully committed to him" (2 Chronicles 16:9), and my heart flipped once again.

> *I can look back and clearly see that God was preparing me for one of the greatest blows to come into my life. He is preparing you as well. Never give up on reading God's Word. It is profoundly relevant today. There are countless passages to comfort and guide you. Don't give up! Ask God to open your eyes and ears so that you can understand what He is saying to you. And know this: He will.*

~ 28 ~

So will it be with the resurrection of the dead. The body that is sown is perishable, it is raised imperishable; it is sown in dishonor, it is raised in glory; it is sown in weakness, it is raised in power; it is sown a natural body, it is raised a spiritual body.

If there is a natural body, there is also a spiritual body.
—1 Corinthians 15:42-44

It was a clear, beautiful, humidity-free morning in New Mexico. The sky was blue, the breeze was soft, and Trip and I had a lovely day planned together. The phone rang, and my mother's voice was strained and crying. "Your daddy's dead. He's dead. Your daddy's dead."

I ran screaming to Trip with the phone still in my hand. "My daddy's dead. He's dead!" And then came the realization in my heart as I remembered the terrible fight I had with my dad the day before. He had high blood pressure and refused to take his medicine. He would get dizzy and then call Trip for help for his inner ear. I remember shouting, "You have to take your blood pressure medicine! It is not your inner ear! Your blood pressure is too high." Livid, I hung up the phone. Guess I told him all right.

And now he was dead. My last words were shouts and accusations. "Oh Trip," I cried, "I fought with him! I screamed at him!" My husband was as calm as anyone I have ever remembered. He looked at me, and said, "Be glad you were not co-dependent with him. Know in your heart that you did everything you could to help him take his medicine, and you did it because you loved him." With that, my inner terror subsided, but the pain and sorrow would be with me for months.

There were so many strange and unusual things that happened to me after my papa died. He was taken from us so suddenly that I felt his spirit was still with us for a time after his passing.

It was the day of his funeral. I got a hotel room for my daughter and myself. We couldn't bear to stay at my parents' home. It was just too sad. We both kept a red rose from his casket. Mine was so precious to me. That night, I laid it gently on a table next to my bed, but the next morning, that rose was on the floor. How did it move by itself? There were no breezes, and I had not been up at all during the night.

My family had a standing joke about Papa's terrible table manners. It was nothing for him to reach past you to fork a biscuit or potato—right past your nose! The Thanksgiving after his passing, my son-in-law and I were shopping at a nearby mall. We were looking over small "gag" gifts on a display table when I spied a fork. "What could this be?" I remember asking Brad. Just then, we both watched as this fork extended about twelve inches, past Brad's nose! We both looked wide-eyed at each other and had that feeling that Papa was near, reaching to fork a biscuit!

The redheaded woodpecker was Papa's favorite bird. I saw more of them after his death than I had ever seen in my life. Even now, when a redheaded woodpecker comes to me, more comes than a bird.

That first Christmas was such a sad time for all of us. We decided to take the family skiing at our condo at Wintergreen resort. I asked my mother to stand on the deck so I could get a picture of her; when she turned around, the air around her was suddenly filled with tiny ice crystals. They swirled and danced all around her sad face. Was Papa near us in spirit?

Thunder snow was something I had never heard before in my life. Sitting at my daughter's that winter, a loud crash brought a flurry of snow pelting the windows. Papa always loved snow, and we were convinced he was nearby in spirit.

Snow came out of nowhere one winter evening in New Mexico. The flakes danced all around me. As I let the flakes fall on my hands and face, I felt his spirit so strongly.

One day in New Mexico, I was feeling particularly sad at his loss. When he would visit, he always stayed in an upstairs bedroom at our house. I slowly climbed the steps, crying softly, begging God to help me, "Lord, help me find something that was his. I need something to hold—something to keep." I started frantically going through drawers and looking under chairs: "a toothbrush, a comb, anything Lord."

I opened the door to a deep clothes closet. On my knees, I crawled in the dark to the very back, turned, and sat crying all alone. I put my hand down by my side and felt something—what could this be? I climbed out of the closet and looked, and it was one of my papa's socks. I knew it was his because it had a familiar hole in the heel! "Thank you, Lord! Thank you for this gift of my papa. He lives! Thank you for letting him come to me!"

I had a vivid dream about six months after he passed; my papa came to me in that dream. He looked so happy. He had the biggest grin on his face I have ever seen. His body had no form, but instead was wispy, reminding me of a breeze. He didn't say a word, but I have never seen him so happy in my life. The next morning I called my mother, "Papa came to me last night in a dream." She replied, "He came to me too." She had seen the same image of him. After that night, I never felt his presence again. I never saw any images of him or had anything unusual happen after that. I knew he was gone. His spirit had left this world.

I am convinced that God allowed him to stay long enough to encourage me and let me know that he did not die that cold, lonely night. He lives and is waiting for me in a heavenly place. Thank you, Lord. Thank you for the peace that only you can bring.

~ 29 ~

*"You will seek me and find me when you seek me with
all your heart. I will be found by you," declares the* LORD,
*"and will bring you back from captivity. I will gather you
from all the nations and places where I have banished
you," declares the* LORD, *"and will bring you back to the
place from which I carried you into exile."*
—Jeremiah 29:13-14

I am convinced God can change the way you look at
situations and environments in order to get your attention.
It's like putting on and taking off "rose-colored glasses."

When I first moved to New Mexico, I remember
thinking it was the most beautiful place on earth! Yes,
I know, it was flat and sandy, but the sky was majestic.
You could see forever and watch storms billow up, rising
on the horizon. The night skies were dark, brilliant with
twinkling stars and gigantic moons. I loved the dry heat
(every day was a good hair day in New Mexico) and the
way the desert would cool down at night. For nearly
five years, I was completely happy with this land of
enchantment. Then things began to change. I couldn't
find peace in the openness. Suddenly, I didn't find
beauty in the sand or the skies, but, instead, a kind of
loneliness and emptiness. It was as if God had changed
the lenses of my glasses. This world didn't appeal to
me. It was time to go home.

An offer came in from a physician recruiter in a place called Wytheville, Virginia. I realized that it wasn't far from Winston Salem, North Carolina. I had never been to Wytheville but at least it was near my home. And Virginia was always so appealing to me, with its mountains and seashores.

We flew into Greensboro, and I remember seeing in the far distant horizon an image of Pilot Mountain in Mount Airy. My heart flipped. This was a nostalgic picture in my mind. I was coming home. We got into our rental car, and as we left the Greensboro-Winston Salem area and headed up the winding road toward Fancy Gap in the Blue Ride Mountains, I began to cry. "I don't know where Wytheville is located, but I know it's home. I'm home, Papa. I'm finally home."

Trip accepted the offer, and we made plans to move back across the country. The moving truck came and left with our furniture. That last night in New Mexico, we slept with our cats and dogs on the floor of the living room. At the crack of dawn, we headed toward the East Coast.

As we were leaving Hobbs, I remember seeing an elderly, gray-haired man walking along the side of the road. He looked just like my papa. My heart sank in a melancholic sorrow. "Oh, Papa. I am so sorry I came out here. I am sorry I left you; and now that I'm coming home, you have left me."

It was a long ride across multiple states. But when I saw "Welcome to Memphis," I knew we had made the right decision. I was and am such a Southern Belle that the very act of crossing that bridge into Memphis thrilled me to my bones.

I was finally back home in the South, within driving distance of the Blue Ridge Mountains. I don't question why I ever left. God had a purpose much grander than I could ever imagine. If I had not been to New Mexico, I would not have heard that life coach on television or had a chance to work with the women in drug court.

It may be in the desert of your life that you begin to search for life's meaning and purpose. It may take a place of overwhelming loss to ever know God's profound love so intimately. Only when I realized that was I ready for Him to bring me home again. Only then could I clearly hear His call.

~ 30 ~

"I am the vine; you are the branches. If you remain in me and I in you, you will bear much fruit; apart from me you can do nothing."

—*John 15:5*

Once I was "back home" in Virginia, I just *had* to do something for women. Almost driven, I began to dream of holding a women's retreat. I would make it memorable and use every trick I had ever learned at the retreats I had attended.

With a beautiful view of the New River from an ancient old farmhouse, the Methodist youth camp looked like the perfect place for a retreat. The camp director was so accommodating. He introduced me to the camp's personal chef. It couldn't get any better! I had a venue and personal chef to create delicious, healthy meals. How good could this be? The beds were a little sparse, and the mattresses had thick, rubber coverings, but the fireplace in the living room would be the perfect place to sip coffee early in the morning when the frost glistened on the grounds!

I purchased all sorts of surprises. The women had to have memorabilia to keep and fresh flowers to take home. I studied scriptures and dug out devotionals that had once spoken to me.

My friend, Phyllis, showed up with a car full of beautiful stemware, plates, cups, and serving pieces. "I found them at a local thrift store! If these women are going to be at a youth camp, at least they can have fine dinnerware."

There were clues along the way about this retreat. As hard as I advertised, my response rate was dismal. I would have three, then four ladies interested, and then the number dropped to two.

My first mistake was the fact that I had not asked God about this retreat. I neither asked nor waited on any direction. This was *my* idea, and I plowed through it. Every minute through the day would be planned. From yoga to music to candles to devotions, I had this thing.

The day arrived and my two ladies arrived. Two wonderful ladies who wanted a place to get away and get close to God. Problem was, I was in the way. Orchestrating every last minute, I must have nearly driven those two ladies crazy. Surely they were completely exhausted after two days at camp with me. I never gave them one minute with the Lord. We had yoga and drills and projects to create. We had to journal and paint and glue our journey onto poster boards. What was I thinking?

I never heard from those ladies again.

I sat down with the Lord—a little late to fix the past, but always in time for the future. I came to know that it was not my job to direct this retreat. This was the Lord's retreat. The ladies were there to hear from Him and not me. If I had prayed and sat and listened, I know that I would have had little to say, and we would have had less "to do." The silence and the beauty of the retreat space alone would have been enough.

It was on my knees scrubbing the toilets after it was all over that I cried out to the Lord, "Lord, it's ok with me if all I do is scrub toilets. I'll do anything you ask me to do, and I will give you praise for whatever my assignment. I'm sorry that this didn't go so well."

And then, a light came on in the darkness. Slowly, it began to dawn on me.

God wanted to help those two women through me. He had it all planned, and I got in the way. But, true to His Word, He uses all things for good. He took my mistake and used it to teach me His way for the future.

It was His power and purpose that brought me to the camp retreat. It was His calling that brought the women. If I had just been still and listened, how different it could have been. For one thing, I wouldn't have been so absolutely frazzled trying to control every minute. The control was His.

My only job was to love them and welcome them. It was mine to create the space for the Lord to do His work.

"Create a space for women to come—a trusting place . . . a nurturing place." I had almost forgotten those words He said to me until I saw Faith House.

~ 31 ~

Praise be to the God and Father of our Lord Jesus Christ, the Father of compassion and the God of all comfort, who comforts us in all our troubles, so that we can comfort those in any trouble with the comfort we ourselves have received from God.
—2 Corinthians 1:3-4

We came down a short hill, and I saw this house. I had remembered seeing the house years before, when my husband and I rented a small home by the river, right next door. There didn't seem to be anything special about her at the time. In fact, I thought she was sort of plain and boring. An odd shape, "must have been a store at some point," with a false front that lifted her facade three stories high.

But this time, she stood in quiet reverence. There was something like a magnet that drew me forward in my seat. "Wait a minute. This house is the house. This is the place that God called me to create a place for women to come!" My realtor looked delighted, while my husband rolled his eyes and shook his head. Gleefully, my steps quickened. It was cold the day we drove up and even colder inside the house. "Must not have the heat turned on," I muttered, "I'll bet she's winterized."

I was in love. I could imagine women coming and sitting around the small decorative wood stove. Three bedrooms would be just enough! I could get two ladies in this one and maybe even four in the front bedroom. I looked around, and my husband was headed back to the car. "Don't worry!" I told my realtor, "I'll work on him."

It was quiet on the way home. I continued to talk about the water that surrounded the house. I knew that would be a seller to Trip. Having grown up in Florida, he loves water. Several nights later, my realtor once again called. "Have you made up your minds on this house? The bad news is that there is going to be an open house there tomorrow, and all of the area realtors are coming to see her."

"Oh No!" I cried to the Lord, "I need some more time. This house is such a charmer that she will surely be sold to someone. I haven't had time to talk Trip into it!" Late that night, the Lord sent an ice storm—the likes of which you have never seen! I mean it was a storm that brewed up from nowhere. About an inch of ice covered the ground the next morning. That real estate open house was called off.

More time! I had more time! We have to go back over and see this house again! All the way over there, Trip complained, "What do we know about an old house? We have never had an old house. We don't know anything about a septic tank, and we know nothing about a well. Besides, you can't heat that old house with those tall ceilings." The realtor met us again. When she opened the door, the warm air pushed out and over us! The house was as warm as toast! Somebody must have turned on the heat! And, just as we were leaving, a pick-up truck stopped in the driveway. A tall, friendly man got out and introduced himself. He said, "I caretake this old house. I know all about the septic tank and the well." I looked at my realtor, and said, "Do you see how the Lord works?" She said, "I DO NOW!" It was another quiet ride home, but the Lord was working!

Then, the inspection report came in. It was thirty-two pages long. I sat down at my kitchen table and thought, "How will I ever get Trip to go along with this?" A name popped in my head. Yes, I'll call my friend who is a contractor! I'll show him the report and see what he says! Doug came by that week and slowly looked through each and every page. I swallowed hard, waiting on an estimate. "This is nothing. They have put down every loose screw on this report. I can take care of all of this for you. Won't be much at all!" Lord! We are still in the game!

But then, the termite report came. She had termites. But by this time I was stepping out in faith. God had a plan for this house, and nothing and no one could stop it! The seller paid for the termite treatment, and the house had no structural damage.

Then, the bank called. "We have some trouble with your mortgage request. It seems this house is in a flood plain, and we probably cannot loan you the money"

"Now what, Lord? This is a big one." I stepped out in faith and had a flood evaluation study done. The report came back, and FEMA had made a mistake! The house should have never been placed in a flood plain!!

We were on a roll! It was time to close the deal! The date and time were set to sign the papers. I went to the bank that morning to get my certified check for the down payment, and every computer in that bank shut down. I looked at the teller, and said, "Don't worry. They'll be back up." And, in minutes—they were!

Even when I was struggling for a name for this house, God came through. Late during the night, I was awake, thinking I could call her "Serenity" or "Peace"—something maybe with water. And, as my head hit the pillow, I heard the word "Faith." Of course! Her name is Faith! How wonderful it will be to say: "Come to Faith" "Never a charge to come to Faith" "Faith is always there for you."

> *Our God is so merciful and loves us beyond what we can imagine. No matter what wrong turn I took in my life, by His compassion and grace, He turned it all for good. Despite my lack of self-esteem, the shame of my birthmark, through my mother's distance and my father's drinking, God never left me.*

> *He followed me through my endless search, looking for love in all the wrong places. He led me out of the desert of addiction, affairs, abortions, and eating disorders.*

> *Even when rejected by a "Christian" colleague, He was there. Never giving up on me, God led me to my purpose in life. Now I am ready. After suffering much pain and loneliness, I want to comfort those with the comfort I myself have received.*

> *Never, ever underestimate the power of purpose. When God calls you, and you have faith to step out and follow Him, there will be nothing you can't do!*

I am humbled that God would call me to help Him. And, to think, He could use the likes of someone like me. Well, maybe He knew I'd be just the one.

Faith House

The table is set Lord and all are welcomed.
Bring those who want normal.
Bring those with alcoholic fathers.
Bring those with absent mothers
    and those who were absent themselves.
Bring those who were abused as children
    and those whose children have been abused.
Bring the adulteress and the addicted.
Bring those who had abortions, separations, and divorce.
Bring those rejected and uninvited.
Bring those who doubt and wonder.
Faith is that place where women can come.
She is a trusting and nurturing place.
All are accepted. All are loved, and all are finally home.

Acknowledgments

Thanks be to God the Father of our Lord Jesus Christ who would not leave me alone until this book was completed. When I wouldn't listen or needed a nudge, He sent those folks into my life who inspired me and encouraged me every step of the way.

To my husband, Trip, who with God's grace has enabled me to do the work of Jesus Christ. My daughter, Jami, who still loves me despite myself.

To my editor, Barbara Dick, who pushed me out of my self-limited box and Latan Murphy who taught me and believed in me from the very start.

I give thanks to God for Donna Waybright, Jill Steele, Debbie Gardner, Desmond Barrett, Beth Lovingood, Bonnie Walker and the entire congregation of Jordan's and Cecil's Chapel for being those friends that you can always fall back on when you begin to self doubt.

And to Phyllis Clabough, my Aaron and Hur, always holding me up when I didn't have the strength to stand.

God has blessed me with so many people who have inspired me, supported me, believed in me and encouraged me to write this book. I can't possibly list all the names on this page but I will hold their names up to Our Lord and ask for His blessings on their lives.

This book also represents the completion of my second year covenant project for The Academy for Spiritual Formation through The Upper Room.

All Glory to God!

Made in the USA
Columbia, SC
10 March 2019